Pandas

Published by Wildlife Education, Ltd.
12233 Thatcher Court, Poway, California 92064
contact us at: 1-800-477-5034
e-mail us at: animals@zoobooks.com
visit us at: www.zoobooks.com

ISBN 1-888153-32-6

Giant Pandas

Created and Written by
John Bonnett Wexo

Scientific Consultant
Dr. George B. Schaller, Ph.D.
Director of New York Zoological Society
International Conservation Program
Co-Director, World Wildlife Fund
Giant Panda Project

Art Credits

Page Eight: Richard Orr; **Page Nine: Upper Right,** Walter Stuart; **Lower Center,** Richard Orr; **Page Ten: Center,** Richard Orr; **Lower Left,** Walter Stuart; **Page Eleven: Upper Right, Center Right, and Lower Left,** Walter Stuart; **Lower Right,** Richard Orr; **Page Twelve:** Walter Stuart; **Page Thirteen: Upper Right,** Walter Stuart; **Lower Center,** Richard Orr; **Pages Sixteen and Seventeen:** Richard Orr; **Page Eighteen: Left Center,** Walter Stuart; **Center Right,** Richard Orr; **Page Nineteen:** Top Center, Walter Stuart; **Lower Center,** Richard Orr

Photographic Credits

Cover: Tim Davis *(Photo Researchers)*; **Pages Six and Seven:** Zig Leszczynski *(Animals Animals)*; **Page Nine: Top Left,** Med Beauregard; **Page Eleven: Top Center,** Tim Rautert *(Bruce Coleman, Ltd.)*; **Lower Center,** Med Beauregard; **Page Twelve: Top Right,** Courtesy of National Zoological Park; **Center,** Howard Quigley; **Lower Right,** Med Beauregard; **Page Thirteen:** Howard Quigley; **Pages Fourteen and Fifteen:** Norman Myers *(Bruce Coleman, Inc.)*; **Page Sixteen:** Tom McHugh *(Photo Researchers)*; **Page Seventeen: Top Left,** George Schaller; **Center Right,** Phillipa Scott; **Page Eighteen: Top Left,** Zoological Society of San Diego; **Top Right,** Jessie Cohen *(National Zoo)*; **Lower Left,** Atlas Dragesco *(Bavaria Verlag)*; **Pages Twenty and Twenty-one:** George Holton *(Photo Researchers)*; **Pages Twenty-two and Twenty-three:** Peter B. Kaplan *(FPG Int'l)*

Contents

Giant Pandas are among the most beautiful and rare animals in the world. They are near the top of almost everybody's list of favorite animals. Whenever there are Giant Pandas in a zoo, people flock to see them.

It's easy to see why they are so popular. They look like big and cuddly Teddy bears, with soft black-and-white fur. They seem friendly and harmless, and even a little helpless at times. It almost seems like Giant Pandas were *made* for people to love.

Giant Pandas can be large animals, as their name implies. When fully grown, they can be almost 5 feet long, and they usually weigh over 200 pounds. The biggest Giant Panda ever weighed was almost 400 pounds. But Giant Pandas aren't really giants in the same way that an elephant is a giant. One average elephant weighs more than *thirty* Giant Pandas.

All of the wild Giant Pandas in the world live in western China. They are found in dense bamboo forests high up in the mountains. The forests are so dense that it has always been hard for people to find out much about wild pandas. The pandas stay hidden in the forest most of the time, where people can't even see them. In many ways, the Giant Panda is still a mysterious animal.

The Chinese people are very proud that these beautiful animals are found only in their country. They have even made the Giant Panda a symbol for their country, in the same way that the Bald Eagle is a symbol for the United States. The Chinese call the Giant Panda *daxiong mao* (dah-shohng mah-oo), which means "large cat-bear."

The people of China are doing many things to protect their Giant Pandas. They have set aside areas of wild land as panda reserves. Chinese scientists are working with scientists from other countries to find out more about wild pandas. And it is against the law in China to harm a Giant Panda in any way.

Many zoos would like to have pandas because they are so popular with zoo visitors. But only a few zoos outside China are allowed to have them, because they are an endangered species.

Giant Pandas look like fun. Their beautiful black-and-white fur looks almost like a costume for a party. Their round ears and the black patches around their eyes make them look like delightful circus clowns.

Giant Pandas have very flexible bodies. They can twist and turn in many directions. They love to do somersaults—over and over and over again. They usually move very slowly. And sometimes they will stop in the middle of a roll and hold a pose for a long time. In zoos, they often play for hours with big rubber balls, plastic hoops, metal barrels, and other toys.

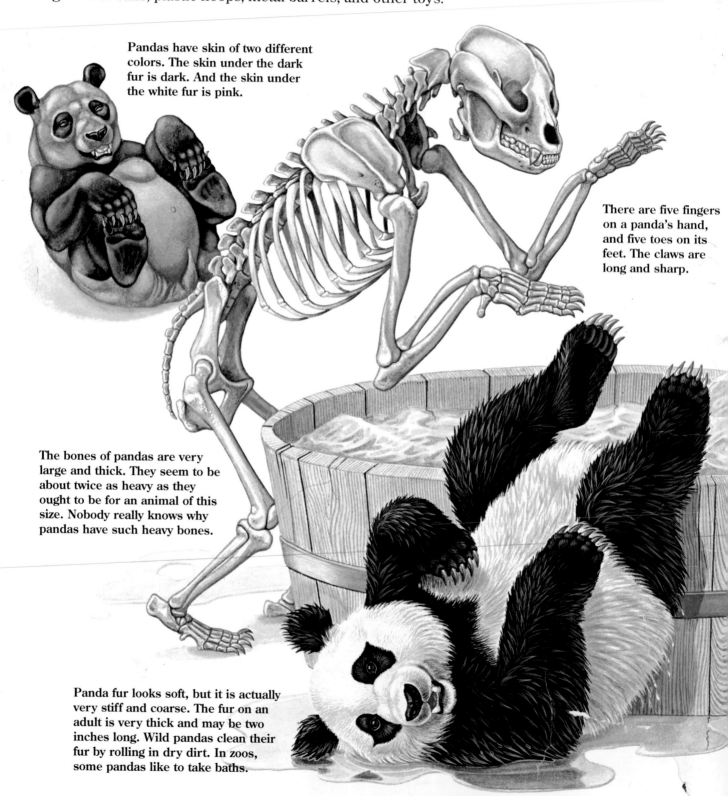

Pandas have skin of two different colors. The skin under the dark fur is dark. And the skin under the white fur is pink.

There are five fingers on a panda's hand, and five toes on its feet. The claws are long and sharp.

The bones of pandas are very large and thick. They seem to be about twice as heavy as they ought to be for an animal of this size. Nobody really knows why pandas have such heavy bones.

Panda fur looks soft, but it is actually very stiff and coarse. The fur on an adult is very thick and may be two inches long. Wild pandas clean their fur by rolling in dry dirt. In zoos, some pandas like to take baths.

People love Giant Pandas for many of the same reasons that they love human babies. Like babies, pandas look friendly and helpless. Like babies, they look round and cuddly. It often seems like they are just waiting for you to hug them. Pandas also have large, flat faces like babies. And they seem to have very big eyes. (The eyes aren't actually that big, but the black patches around them make them *look* big.) Pandas are also very playful like babies. They often do things that are just plain *cute*.

BIG FACE

BIG EYES

LOOKS FRIENDLY

ROUND AND CUDDLY

Stuffed panda toys and Teddy bears are probably the two most popular toys of all time. Millions of children have owned them and loved them. This may be one reason why so many people love real pandas and bears.

The front part of a panda's body is very strong. Pandas in zoos usually destroy their toys very quickly. Even the strongest toys are no match for a panda's strong hands and jaws.

The rear legs of pandas are not as strong as the front legs. This may be one reason why pandas don't seem able to run very fast. Even when they are being chased, pandas never move faster than a slow trot.

9

Bamboo is the most important thing in a wild panda's life. In fact, the life of a panda actually *depends* on bamboo—because bamboo is the main food that pandas eat. Some scientists say that *99 percent* of all the food a wild panda eats is bamboo.

The panda's name may even be based on its fondness for bamboo. Some people believe that the word "panda" comes from a native word that means "bamboo eater."

Bamboo plants are really *grass* that can grow as tall as trees. There are hundreds of different kinds of bamboo, but pandas only eat about 20 different kinds. Most of the time, they eat only 4 or 5 kinds that are most plentiful in areas where they live.

Everywhere a panda goes in a bamboo forest, it is surrounded by food. To eat, all it has to do is sit down and grab a nearby stalk of bamboo. Sitting in one place, it can bend dozens of stalks into its mouth. With very little effort, it can chew on more than 3,400 bamboo stalks *every day*. Very few animals have such an easy time getting their food.

Every day, a panda can eat an incredible amount of bamboo. Most pandas spend up to 16 hours a day eating. They eat for a while, sleep for a while, and then eat some more. They may even eat in the middle of the night. In one year, a panda can eat more than *10,000 pounds* of bamboo.

Pandas seem to prefer to eat tender bamboo shoots and leaves when they can get them. But they also eat large stalks up to 1½ inches thick. The outer covering of these stalks is very hard. Pandas strip it away with their teeth and eat the softer pith inside.

To help it grab bamboo, a Giant Panda has unusual "hands." Like a human hand, the panda's hand has a special "thumb" that makes it possible to grab things very tightly. In fact, the Giant Panda is one of the few large animals that can grab things as tightly as a human can. But the panda's "thumb" works in a different way from a human thumb, as explained below.

The panda's "thumb" is not really a thumb at all. It is a large wrist bone called a *radial sesamoid* (ray-dee-uhl sess-uh-moid) bone. And a panda does not wrap its "thumb" around things to hold them, as humans do ①. Instead, the panda wraps its five fingers around one side of a bamboo stalk ②. Then it pushes the radial sesamoid bone forward ③ to jam the bamboo against the fingers.

PANDA TEETH

To chew bamboo, pandas have very big teeth. The teeth are wide and thick. They crush the bamboo and grind it up. Like humans, pandas get two sets of teeth—a baby set and an adult set. There are 42 teeth in the mouth of an adult panda. As you can see, the cheek teeth of a panda (above) are about seven times bigger than the human cheek teeth (below).

HUMAN TEETH

The whole head of the panda is a giant machine for crushing bamboo. The jaws are made of very strong, thick bone. And the huge cheek muscles can close the jaws with tremendous force. A thick stalk of bamboo is so hard that you would have trouble breaking it with an axe. But a panda can crush it easily and chew it to bits.

PITH

OUTER COVERING

Pandas sometimes eat other things besides bamboo. When they can get it, they will eat meat. And they seem to be very fond of honey. They also eat grass, vines, and roots. In the spring, they may even eat flowers.

Giant Pandas can only live in places where there is enough bamboo for them to eat. And the kinds of bamboo that pandas prefer to eat are found high up in the mountains, where it can get very cold.

During the coldest part of the winter, there are often many feet of snow on the ground. But no matter how cold it gets, the bamboo stays green— and the pandas keep eating it. Unlike bears, pandas do not sleep in dens during the winter. They continue to wander through the snowy bamboo forests, eating as they go.

Like other animals that live in cold places, pandas seem to like the cold. In zoos, pandas are often given blocks of ice to cool them off when the weather gets hot. Many times, they will lie down on the ice and go happily to sleep.

The bamboo grows so thick in panda country that it is often impossible for people to make their way through it. Pandas can crawl under the bamboo thickets and wriggle between tightly packed bamboo stalks, but people can't. For this reason, scientists who want to study wild pandas must often capture them first. To do this, they bait a trap with meat, as shown at left. When a panda goes inside to get the meat, the door slides shut.

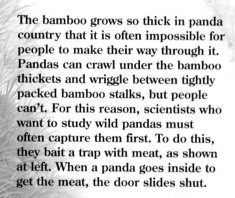

Scientists put the trapped panda to sleep with a harmless drug. While the panda sleeps, it is weighed and examined. The scientists look at the amount of wear on the teeth, because this indicates the age of the animal. They check to see whether the panda has any diseases, and give it medicine if needed. Finally, they attach a radio collar to the panda's neck.

The radio collar is very strong and waterproof. It will keep sending signals for a year or more. The collar does not hurt the panda in any way.

Once the collar is firmly attached, the panda is allowed to wake up and is released into the forest. As it wanders away, the radio collar sends out signals. Scientists can use the radio signals to find out where the panda goes in the dense forest.

Bamboo grows best in places where there is a lot of water. And this is why it grows so well in panda country. During the winter, there is a lot of snow in the mountains—and during the summer there is a lot of rain. More than 50 inches of rain and snow may fall every year.

C H I N A

Thousands of years ago, there were bamboo forests all over eastern China. And for this reason, pandas were able to live in a very large area (orange on the map). But the climate in eastern China has grown drier over the years. And people have also cut down bamboo in many places to make room for farms. As a result, the bamboo forests are much smaller today, and Giant Pandas can only be found in a few small areas (red on the map).

Pandas may play in the snow like children. One scientist found a place where a panda went sledding down a hill on its stomach. It "belly flopped" to the bottom, climbed back up the hill—*and did it again*.

Panda mothers take very good care of their babies. As soon as a baby is born, its mother takes it in her arms like a human mother cuddling her child. The panda mother feeds the baby milk and never lets it out of her sight.

Baby pandas need this kind of protection because they are completely helpless when they are born. And there are animals in the forest that would like to eat them. (Scientists have found evidence that leopards and wild dogs eat young pandas.)

When predators try to attack a young panda, its mother may protect it by biting with her powerful jaws, as shown below. There is no doubt that panda jaws could crush bones as easily as they crush bamboo— although no one has actually seen this happen.

Most baby pandas are born in dens. The dens are often found in hollow trees. Mother and baby are probably very snug in their den, no matter how cold it gets outside.

Chinese Leopards are probably too small to stand up to an angry mother panda. A fully grown panda weighs twice as much as a leopard.

16

Pandas sometimes climb trees to escape from danger. When they are young and small, they can scamper up a tree in no time at all. As they grow older and heavier, it becomes harder for them to climb. But even older pandas will climb trees to find a safe place to sleep.

The powerful jaws of a mother panda can be very gentle when she holds her baby in them. Like a cat, she may pick up her baby by the neck to carry it from place to place.

By the time a young panda is seven months old, it weighs over 20 pounds. It can run and climb trees, and it has started to eat bamboo. Eleven months later, it weighs 120 pounds, and it is ready to leave its mother.

When they are born, baby pandas are tiny. Their mothers are about 900 times bigger than they are. The babies grow rapidly, as shown below. But they stay helpless for a long time. Their eyes don't open until they are about 40 days old. And they can't even crawl until they are about 3 or 4 months old.

FOUR MONTHS OLD
6 ½ pounds

THREE MONTHS OLD

ONE MONTH OLD

NEWBORN
4 ounces

17

Giant Pandas are mysterious. Nobody is really sure what kind of animal they are. Some scientists say that the Giant Panda is a member of the *raccoon* family. But others claim that it belongs to the *bear* family. And a third group is sure that it doesn't belong to *either* family.

Scientists who say that Giant Pandas are raccoons try to prove it by showing that the Giant Panda is closely related to a small animal called the *Red Panda*. Many people believe that the Red Panda belongs to the raccoon family. So, if the Giant Panda and the Red Panda are related, and the Red Panda is a raccoon. . . well, the Giant Panda must also be a raccoon.

But scientists who claim that Giant Pandas are bears don't agree that the Giant Panda and the Red Panda are closely related. As you will see on these pages, there seem to be plenty of facts to prove that giant pandas are bears. . . or maybe raccoons. . . or maybe something else. It's all very confusing.

BEAR

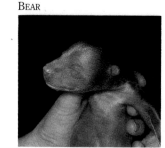

Giant Pandas may be *bears* because. . .
Newborn bears and newborn Giant Pandas look very much alike. Both are very tiny compared to their parents, and both are covered with very fine hair.

GIANT PANDA

Red Pandas live in the same part of the world as Giant Pandas. They are found high up in the mountains in the same bamboo forests.

The pattern on the face of a Red Panda looks very much like the pattern on the face of a Giant Panda, with patches around the eyes.

ASIATIC BLACK BEAR
Selenarctos thibetanus

RACCOON
Procyon lotor

RED PANDA
Ailurus fulgens

18

Giant Pandas may be *raccoons* because. . .

The teeth of giant pandas and red pandas are very much alike. And the teeth of giant pandas are very *different* from bear teeth. Bears have narrow teeth that are made for cutting and chewing. But giant pandas and red pandas have wide teeth that are made for crushing bamboo.

GIANT PANDA

RED PANDA

POLAR BEAR

The scientific evidence is *confusing*. . .

Some blood tests have indicated that Giant Pandas are more closely related to bears than to Red Pandas. But studies of panda genetics seem to show that the Giant Panda is most closely related to the Red Panda.

Giant Pandas may be *bears* because. . .

Giant pandas look like bears. They have big round bodies like bears, and big round heads. The ears on Giant Pandas even look like the ears of Asiatic Black Bears, which live in the same part of the world.

GIANT PANDA
Ailuropoda melanoleuca

Giant Pandas may not be bears or raccoons because. . .

Giant Pandas sit down to eat their food, but bears and Red Pandas do not. And only the Giant Panda has special "thumbs" for grabbing things tightly.

Giant Pandas may be *raccoons* because. . .

Red Pandas and Giant Pandas both eat a lot of bamboo. They bring the bamboo up to their mouths in a similar way. And they use their teeth to strip off the hard outer covering of the bamboo in a similar way.

19

Unlike Giant Pandas, Red Pandas usually live in groups. There may be three or more of them living together. And Red Pandas seem to spend much more time up in trees than Giant Pandas do. They usually come down to the ground to eat, but climb back up when they are finished.

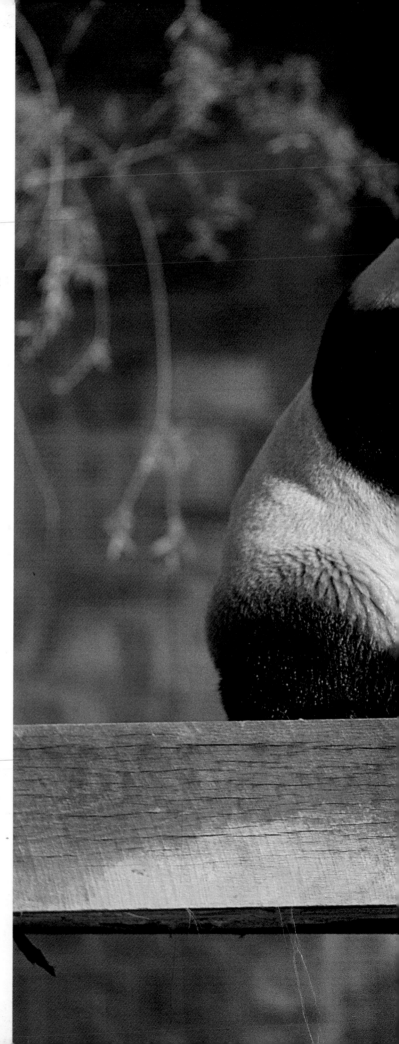

The future of Giant Pandas is hard to predict. They are already among the most endangered animals on earth, and their numbers are very small. Scientists believe that there may be less than 1,000 Giant Pandas still living in the mountains of western China.

To survive, these wild pandas will need enough land to live on, and enough bamboo to eat. The Chinese government has already done a great deal to help give the pandas these things. Large areas have been set aside as panda reserves—and these areas contain some of the best bamboo forest remaining in China.

But the pandas are still not totally safe. There are people living in some of the reserves, and they want to cut down more bamboo to make room for farming. Other people would like to cut down the trees and bamboo in the forest to build houses.

The most serious danger for pandas may come from the *bamboo plants* that pandas like to eat. Each kind (or species) of bamboo plant lives and grows for a certain number of years—from 40 to 80 years. Then the bamboo plants of that species flower and die. When one species of bamboo dies, *all* of the bamboo of that kind dies *at the same time*. Entire forests of bamboo may die all at once, leaving the pandas that live in those forests without bamboo to eat.

This happened in 1975, when all of the Umbrella Bamboo died. With nothing to eat, more than 150 Giant Pandas starved to death. In 1983, all of the Arrow Bamboo died, and hundreds of pandas were in danger again. But this time, the Chinese and the World Wildlife Fund were able to help the pandas.

For several years, Chinese scientists and World Wildlife Fund scientists have been studying pandas and their food supply. They hope to learn enough to make sure that wild pandas will always have enough living space and enough to eat. And they want to find ways to increase the number of pandas that are born in the wild and in zoos. If they can do all of these things, the future of Giant Pandas may be bright after all.

If you would like to find out how you can help save the Giant Pandas, write to the World Wildlife Fund, 1250 24th Street N.W., Washington, D.C. 20037.

Index